BORTHWICK INSTITUTE OF HISTORICAL
UNIVERSITY OF YORK

York against Durham:
The Guardianship of the
Spiritualities in the
Diocese of Durham
Sede Vacante

by

Barry Till
Sometime Fellow and Dean of Jesus College, Cambridge

BORTHWICK PAPER No. 84

First Published 1993
© Barry Till

ISSN: 0524-0913

Acknowledgements

One of the pleasures of returning to the groves of academe after an absence of some thirty years is the rediscovery of the kindness and generosity of colleagues who so readily offer guidance and advice.

I stumbled on the excommunication by Archbishop Richard Sterne of his Chancellor Thomas Burwell in 1672 when working on the updating of my previous studies at the Borthwick Institute in York. Dr W. J. (Bill) Sheils was in the Library at the time and I well remember his whistle when I mentioned the bizarre incident. Since then he has been most kind in encouraging this study for publication as a Borthwick Paper. It is fitting that it should appear under the Borthwick imprint, not only because of the subject matter, but because of the guidance I received there in studying the post-Restoration York ecclesiastical courts in the fifties. The present Borthwick generation (led by Dr David Smith) has been equally helpful and I must especially thank Mr Christopher Webb for some valuable suggestions.

In York, too, the Minster Library made its archive available, while more recent authorities in the persons of Provincial Registrars shared their memories with me. To his memory Colonel Innes Ware added his excellent sherry.

In Durham the guardians of the various papers were uniformly kind and helpful – and there can surely be no more beautiful places in which to work. Miss McCollum in the University Library, Mr Roger Norris in the Dean and Chapter Library, and Mr Pat Mussett in the Prior's Kitchen were generous in their guidance and thereby saved me much time. I am grateful to the Dean and Chapter for access to their records and to the Chapter Clerk, Mr Frank Gibbs, for making available to me the most recent Chapter Minute Books. I must also thank the Dean and Chapter for allowing me to quote from their material.

In London most of the work on the background to the Restoration Settlement has been done at that most hospitable of libraries, Dr Williams' in Gordon Square, and I must particularly thank the Assistant Librarian, Mrs Janet Barnes, for her unfailing patience stretching back over many years.

At the Lambeth Palace Library I had the good fortune to be able to draw on the memory of the former Librarian, Dr E. G. W. Bill, who pointed me unerringly at the key manuscript for the whole study. Miss Melanie Barber, the Deputy Librarian and Archivist, helped me on a number of matters.

When it came to examining the abortive attempt to rationalise the *sede vacante* arrangements in the Church of England General Synod in 1975 and 1976 Miss Ingrid Slaughter, Assistant Legal Adviser to the Synod, took immense trouble to locate the relevant documentation, and also suggested amendments to the text.

Dr David Marcombe, of the Centre for Local History at the University of Nottingham, most kindly made available to me the relevant chapter from his

Durham Ph.D. thesis on "The Dean and Chapter of Durham, 1558-1603".

I am grateful to the Bishop of Chichester and to Dr D. M. Carey for permission to quote from their correspondence.

I have to thank my former Cambridge pupil of the fifties, Canon Michael Perry, Archdeacon of Durham, for carefully reading the most recent section of the paper and making available to me material from his knowledge of events and papers to which I was not privy when preparing my first draft. My old friend and former Cambridge colleague, Bishop Hugh Montefiore has been, *more suo*, full of interest and suggestions.

Lastly I am grateful to my daughter Lucy for her patience in helping me to bridge the traumatic gap between a post-war Imperial portable and a new state-of-the-art computer.

York against Durham: The Guardianship of the Spiritualities in the Diocese of Durham Sede Vacante

I

"Nowhere is the basic conservatism of the re-establishment of the Church better seen than in the revival of its judicial authority" wrote Dr E. O. A. Whiteman in 1955 – and her judgement stands today despite the fact that the history of other aspects of the restoration of the church has been substantially revised since that time.[1] The earlier events of the Restoration need not, however, have led inevitably to that conclusion. If the Worcester House Declaration of 25 October 1660 had been implemented the shape and composition of the Church of England (including the administrative and disciplinary machinery of metropolitan and diocesan Chancellors, Officials Principal and Registrars) might have been very different. It is true that the Declaration did not touch specifically on the church courts, but the "small print" additions which were made to the original draft (and which so much delighted Richard Baxter and his fellow negotiators) would have broken the church down into small and more local units – effectively rural deaneries – along the lines of Archbishop Ussher's *Reduction of Episcopacy*, with which Baxter always said he was in perfect agreement and which the Presbyterians had put forward as their negotiating position.[2] On to such a structure the local enforcement of church discipline (with, no doubt, final appeal to diocesan courts) could have been grafted – and undoubtedly would have been had Baxter had any voice in the matter.[3]

But the Declaration was still-born. The Presbyterians seized on it with glee and, against the King's wishes, brought it to the Commons on 6 November

1660. One thing certainly emerged from an inconclusive debate, namely that the Declaration as it stood was not suitable for immediate translation into legislation, either in Parliament or Convocation.[4] However, that next move never took place after the King stepped in and foreclosed the debate.[5] In the words of Dr Bosher it was "the crucial moment in the history of the church settlement."[6]

So ended the reforms proposed in the Worcester House Declaration: all the commentators agree that the Declaration had been the high water mark of the hope of moderate reform in the Church which would have carried with it a wider comprehension of membership, embracing at least the more moderate, and numerically more numerous, Presbyterians in the country.

The next chapter in the Restoration Settlement came in the spring and summer of 1661 with the meetings of the Savoy Conference from 15 April and the referral of the re-establishment of the church to the new – and much more "Anglican" – Cavalier Parliament. On 25 June a Committee was entrusted with the work of "confirming" the Liturgy, preparing a bill to ensure "effectual conformity", and considering legislation on the church courts and particularly the High Commission. This third task was soon separated from the first two and legislation on the church courts (and with them by implication diocesan administration generally) forged ahead with a bill before the Commons on 27 July and the eventual restoration of the courts by 13 Chas II, c. 12. in the autumn. This Act repealed the legislation of the Long Parliament, and restored the courts as they were before the Civil War with the exception that the High Commission was abolished as was the use of the *ex officio* oath, by which suspected parties were forced to answer a case without being told its precise nature, thus running the danger of incriminating themselves under oath. No other reforms were introduced. In particular there were no references to laymen occupying the office of Chancellor, nor to the indiscriminate use of the dread power – as it should have been – of excommunication as part of the ordinary machinery by which the courts carried out their day-to-day business – for instance enforcing attendance – rather than as the ultimate disciplinary judgement of the Church. (It has been estimated that, before the Civil War, five per cent of the total population were "hardened excommunicates", that is living excommunicate for a period of ten years: if their families were added to this figure it could climb as high as fifteen per cent.)[7] These two abuses had been the persistent agenda as the lowest common denominator in Puritan calls for reform throughout the century. They were included in the proposals of the Worcester House Declaration, but to no avail: they were ignored in the later, and definitive, legislation of the autumn of 1661.

In fact, as Spurr comments, "some church courts had gone to work well before this legislation, but now they began to step up their activity." In York the Court of the Dean and Chapter was sitting *sede vacante* as early as 21 August

1660.[8] By April 1661 the Consistory Court was sitting regularly on Thursdays, and was especially busy with tithe cases, as was to be expected after the chaos of the Interregnum. It is clear however that the courts were to some extent toothless: until legalised by the legislation in the autumn they could only declare recalcitrants contumacious: the first excommunication is not noted until 17 November.[9]

The speedy re-establishment of the courts would depend largely on the availability of their key officers, particularly the Chancellor and Registrar. Unusually in the Nottingham Archdeaconry which, though part of the diocese of York, operated a quasi-independent Consistory Court, both officials survived. The pre-war Official was (Sir) Edward Lake, while John Combes was the Registrar. From 12 August 1660 Lake was writing to Combes and on 17 September he confirmed that the Archdeacon could conduct a visitation *sede vacante*. In February 1661 he was sending specific instructions as to how to proceed, though in his absence with administrative rather than judicial matters: licences and inductions were in order but his surrogates were not to "use corrective power but only pronounce contumacious."[10]

York was not so well placed. The Registrar had survived in the person of George Aislabie who was active in diocesan business as early as 26 October 1660.[11] He had been the "servant" of an earlier Registrar and had married his widow, who brought him a substantial fortune to which he added the proceeds of "improving" the office from £500 to £2000 a year.[12] The Chancellorship was, however, vacant since the death of William Easdall in 1640. Archbishop Frewen appointed Thomas Burwell LL.D. who had been Chancellor of Durham since 1632 and did not give up that post. Given the well-known and long-standing hostility between the Archdiocese of York and the princely see of Durham this was a strange appointment, and not simply because of the legal anomaly that in the case of an appeal from Durham to York Burwell could be reviewing his own sentence.[13] Burwell, originally a Peterhouse man, had transferred from Trinity Hall, the Cambridge nursery of civil lawyers, where he was a Fellow from 1626 to 1632. During that period he might have gained some experience of the practice of the church courts, as many of his peers did, by acting as an advocate, or even a proctor, in the Ely Consistory Court which sat in Great St Mary's, Cambridge. He was appointed to Durham at the age of about forty. He did not receive his LL.D. until 1660. The following year he entered the Cavalier Parliament by the interest of the Archbishop as Member for Ripon. He remained an MP until his death in March 1673. He is described as "a very active Committee man" serving on no fewer than 126 committees, which must have meant that while Parliament was sitting he was pretty much tied to London. Many of these committees were, naturally enough, those which concerned ecclesiastical affairs; for instance on 17 March 1668 he defended the jurisdiction of the ecclesiastical courts when they were under attack in the Commons, as was not uncommon. He also strongly resisted the enfranchisement of Durham as being against the Prince Bishop's interests. He is described as a "moderate", but shortly before his death he pronounced in Parliament that "a Puritan was ever a rebel."[14] Yet until his death Burwell continued to sit regularly, if not frequently, in both the York and Durham courts. It seems probable that his residence remained in Durham: he had married the step-daughter of the Dean of Durham in 1633 and there is a surviving uncatalogued note to his York housekeeper enjoining her to have his bed well aired against his visit, which suggests that York was not his home.

There were three principal grounds for friction between York and Durham, all of which would involve the Chancellor and which might have given Frewen pause in appointing Burwell to York without insisting that the relinquish his Durham post.

The first was the fact that the Bishop of Durham was seized of jurisdiction in substantial areas within the boundaries of the diocese of York, principally in the Peculiars of Allerton and Howden – the latter some 25 miles south-east of York and bordering the Humber. This complication had already got Burwell into trouble. In 1638 or 1639 he was summoned before the High Commission in York for infringing the jurisdiction of the York Prerogative Court from the Allerton Peculiar by failing to enquire under oath whether an estate had *bona notabilia* in more than one jurisdiction and calling testamentary cases to his court rather than to the Prerogative Court in York. The Articles in the case concluded that when he was warned about this Burwell had replied he "would answer and try it with Dr Leggatt, the judge of the Exchequer."[15] Burwell had thus demonstrated his hostility while at Durham to the York jurisdiction; but evidently by 1660 the incident was forgiven – or forgotten.

The question of the geographically overlapping jurisdiction administered by Durham within the territories of the York diocese was one *casus belli* between York and Durham. There were two more, even more serious and potentially explosive. Both reach back through the Middle Ages and are buttressed by a formidable array of decrees, judgements and settlements variously supporting each of the disputants. The first concerns the right of the Metropolitan to carry out a Visitation of the diocese of Durham as he could and did in the other two dioceses of his Province. This right was usually stoutly resisted and thefore not often invoked in the Middle Ages: on one occasion a rash Archbishop narrowly escaped with his life in Durham. In fact "Edward II, Edward III and Henry IV had all issued prohibitions under the Great Seal against archiepiscopal visitations of Durham."[16] More recently, in 1573, Archbishop Edwin Sandys had attempted a visitation while there was a bishop in office in Durham, "an unheard-of encroachment upon Palatinate privilege", and one where insult was added to injury because Bishop Richard Barnes of Durham consented to act as Sandys' agent in the visitation.[17] What is important in this context is that it was the Dean and Chapter of Durham who led the opposition to the visitation as champions of the ancient rights and privileges of the Palatinate. Matters came to a head when the Bishop attempted to visit the Cathedral to be met by a locked Chapter House door and a brief scuffle with Dean Whittingham. Bishop Barnes took the only course open to him and excommunicated the Chapter, while Archbishop Sandys summoned the Dean and most of the prebends before the High Commission in York. In their turn the Dean and Chapter appealed to the Court of Delegates, the highest ecclesiastical court in the country – the second time in two years that a York/ Durham dispute had led to the convening of that court.[18] The case dragged on for four years, partly because of the difficulty of gathering a quorum of the busy Delegates appointed for such an important trial. After an optimistic start the Dean and Chapter found their hopes on the wane and the case was dropped. Later Bishop Barnes – older and wiser – was to regret his agreement to the visitation when in 1584 he "came to a better understanding of the rights and privileges of the see."[19]

The third forum of dispute was equally ancient and even more intractable. It concerned the rights of the jurisdiction or guardianship of the spiritualities of the see of Durham *sede vacante*. The Archbishop of York claimed the jurisdiction citing the universal custom in other sees in both northern and southern provinces. Against this the Dean and Chapter of Durham insisted that the guardianship of the spiritualities was by ancient prescription theirs.[20] A further twist was added on the (comparatively rare) occasions when both Durham and York were vacant, in which case the York Dean and Chapter claimed the jurisdiction. This controversy had surfaced at regular intervals throughout the Middle Ages with new precedents and extra judgements being added century by century. The final position is summarised by R. B. Dobson: "In the later Middle Ages . . . . as at all times the ultimate test of the attitude of the Church of York to its northern neighbour was the policy it adopted during a vacancy in the see of Durham."[21] A settlement of 2 November 1286 had given York "diocesan jurisdiction *sede vacante* in return for the implied freedom of the diocese (of Durham) from metropolitan visitation *sede plena* . . . . and this proved a viable and lasting compromise" since the Prior and Chapter "usually if reluctantly" conceded the Archbishop's rights *sede vacante*.[22] (The situation in a double vacancy was more complicated, and in 1406 the Durham Prior and Chapter were "completely successful in holding the York Dean and Chapter at bay.")[23]

However the Reformation changed the situation and (again to quote Dobson) the former "grudging monks' concessions" were "shattered by Henry VIII's refoundation of the Dean and Chapter as a secular body" with the result that the Dean and Chapter were "more successful than their Medieval predecessors" in claiming the guardianship of the spiritualities *sede vacante*.[24] The

legal position behind this change will be dicussed later. Meanwhile the
occasions when the matter came to a head between the Reformation and the
Restoration can be briefly described. The Durham Dean and Chapter had
defended their rights at the time of Tunstall's deprivation in 1553 but made no
attempt to do so at Elizabeth's accession in 1560 when both sees were vacant
and the York Dean and Chapter successfully exercised jurisdiction. This
dereliction was later bitterly regretted and renounced, being attributed to the
exceptional post-Marian circumstances and the fact that "there was none at
Durham that durst resist, being all Papists and afraid to stand in any controversy."[25]
This single exception, said the later Dean and Chapter, did not constitute a
prescription. In 1576 both sees were vacant again and conflict broke out
between the two Deans, Hutton of York and Whittingham of Durham. This
was the case, already mentioned, which was appealed by the Durham Chapter
to the Court of Delegates. In the end both sides submitted to the conciliatory
procedure of arbitration by the Earl of Huntingdon who produced a face-
saving compromise. This only lasted while both sees were vacant, and when the
bellicose Archbishop Sandys was appointed to York he immediately put in
hand his claim to the jurisdiction, a claim which was resisted by Durham and
aborted soon after by the election of Bishop Barnes to Durham. The dispute
of 1576 resulted therefore, in a draw, though the lists were re-entered
immediately after by Sandys' metropolitan visitation and the appeal to the
Delegates described above.[26]

The last serious conflict over *sede vacante* jurisdiction – and the judgement
which was to colour all future trials of strength at a Durham vacancy – broke
out at the death of Barnes in 1587. Archbishop Sandys predictably moved at
once, sending two commissioners to Durham who were resisted by the Dean
and Chapter, leading to what can only be described as a "punch-up" and a flurry
of mutual excommunications. A further attempt by Sandys, sending in a new
Commissioner, ended in the same way. Meanwhile the Dean and Chapter had
in October appealed to the Delegates who issued an inhibition against the
Archbishop who withdrew from the fray; the Dean and Chapter assumed the
jurisdiction of the diocese through the regular Chancellor, acting as surrogate
to Dean Matthew who occasionally acted in person. The cause meanwhile
ground through the Delegates, delayed no doubt by the same factors as had
made the 1577 trial so slow. Finally on 30 December 1590 the Delegates found
for York with expenses against Durham.[27]

The Chapter, however, had made its dispositions for such an outcome.
They had engaged the prominent common lawyers Coke and Egerton to
approach Queen's Bench to secure a writ of prohibition. Coke dealt with the
case and the prohibition against the ecclesiastical court (itself a tribunal of
monarch in chancery) was a classic example of the tussle over jurisdiction at this
time when the common law courts were beginning to win back – or encroach

on – the ground of the spiritual – or civil – courts in the name of statute and case law.[28] The Archbishop had foreseen this move by the Dean and Chapter and complained to the Lord Chancellor, Sir Christopher Hatton, that they were likely to appeal to the Queen's Bench. Hatton was briefed about the case and asked to get the Court of Chancery to block the Chapter's move – or else to hear the case himself. To no avail. The Queen herself was said to have prohibited the Queen's Bench from considering York's argument that the cause should revert to the Delegates. In the event it was heard at Queen's Bench and the court found for Durham.[29] A later searcher of the records believed that the jury was recruited from "the county of Northumberland" – a body, one might think, as liable to be prejudiced for Durham as the Court of Delegates may have been for York, since two out of the three Delegates who delivered the verdict, Thomas Binge and Richard Swale,were prebendaries of York.[30]

The Durham Dean and Chapter had emerged victorious. Later commentators believed that in the five ensuing vacancies up to the Restoration they were successful, not only in claiming the jurisdiction – which the Archbishop sometimes also did – but in actually exercising it. In 1628, for instance, when Bishop Neile was translated to Winchester, the Dean and Chapter and the Archbishop had instituted different men to the same living. The case went to the Durham Assizes and was won by the Dean and Chapter.[31] This vacancy was also the one when William Easdall was Chancellor of both Durham and York. The Dean and Chapter were determined to demonstrate which of the two was his master. Before the vacancy he had been required to promise "not to question anything we have already transacted."[32] When the vacancy came they "inhibited him until he took a special commission from them."[33] To complicate matters further the see of York was vacant at the same time and on 28 April 1628 the Dean and Chapter of York appointed Easdall, Edmund Mainwaring and John Lively to exercise the jurisdiction of Durham on their behalf. But evidently Easdall's loyalty was to Durham. Similarly at the next vacancy: on 4 March, 1632 the Durham Dean and Chapter were very insistent that Thomas Burwell and his Registrar, Richard Newhouse, must formally accept their patent for the guardianship of the spiritualities *sede vacante* and give half the fees collected to a nominee of theirs.[34]

At the Restoration itself the Dean and Chapter of Durham were quick to re-assert their rights, drawing the King's attention to their being based on statute law, a fact which Charles acknowledged in a letter to the new bishop which was recorded in the Chapter Act Book in November 1660.[35]

II

This, then, was the *hereditas* into which Thomas Burwell entered when he
accepted Archbishop Frewen's appointment to the York Chancellorship. He
virtually ensured that the *hereditas* was *damnosa* when he failed to resign his
Durham post. But it was some years before the crisis came. Bishop John Cosin
died on 15 January 1672 and the see of Durham was vacant. On 20 January the
Archbishop, Richard Sterne, inhibited the Durham Dean and Chapter from
acting in the vacancy, the certificate being in the name of Christopher Morley
(the York Apparitor General who often acted as the agent in office cases) against
Burwell, his surrogates and Registrar, and against John Sudbury, the Dean of
Durham. There followed a citation for contempt in ignoring the inhibition.
(Meanwhile on 22 January Burwell had received his patent from the Dean and
Chapter as their Commissary). Burwell was thus the defendant in his own court
in an office case brought by the Archbishop. He had time to consider his
position because the cause was not heard until 18 April at Bishopthorpe before
Archbishop Sterne himself, with Aislabie making one of his rare appearances
as Registrar.[36] Burwell and Sudbury both appeared through proctors and
appealed against the inhibition on various technical grounds. Nevertheless on
26 April they were declared contumacious, though the penalty was reserved.
But on 17 May at Bishopthorpe Burwell was excommunicated! This was met
by a prohibition dated 10 May from the Court of King's Bench in London, the
prohibition being based both on the prescription of custom and usage which
favoured Durham and on the verdict against Archbishop Sandys in 1590, which
had never been reversed.[37]

There for the moment the matter rested on the legal front except for one
curious circumstance. It has been seen that, with his parliamentary duties and
his prior loyalty to Durham, Burwell's attendances at York were comparatively
rare. He paid occasional visits but was most likely to sit with any regularity in
the Trinity Term when Parliament would not be sitting and when the hazards
of an unaired bed would presumably be diminished. His place was normally
taken by Philip Broome and Henry Watkinson, his surrogates, who were
advocates in the court and who might therefore be adjudging causes in which
they themselves were involved. Another surrogate, John Levet, sat mainly in
the Exchequer Court. In 1672, however, this pattern changed. Burwell sat on
8 February, within days of Cosin's death, and later in February and throughout
March. After the Easter vacation he resumed regular attendance. He was even
sitting in the Consistory Court on 18 April, the day he was summoned before
the Archbishop at Bishopthorpe.[38] He was also sitting on the next court day,
2 May (though from a crossed out entry Levet had evidently been expected),
and he continued regularly through May, June and July, and after the summer
vacation. Not until January 1673 was the normal pattern of Broome and

Watkinson resumed.[39]

It is true that Burwell was helped in establishing this, for him, eccentric time-table by the fact that Parliament was prorogued from 24 March 1672 to 25 March 1673. But he might have celebrated this reprieve from his parliamentary duties by concentrating on his safer duties at home in Durham. What was the reason for this sudden change in habits of twelve years' standing? He can hardly have hoped to curry favour at this stage with the Archbishop. More likely it was the bravado of an old man, coupled with an attempt to re-establish his authority in his courts. After 3 October 1672 the Consistory and Chancery Courts sat together in his presence, which may, again, have been part of a plan to concentrate his authority.[40]

In the New Year of 1673 he was absent – sitting in Durham – but he was in fact attending Parliament on the day before his death at the end of March.[41] Easter followed, and then on Saturday 24 May 1673, at Bishopthorpe, in the presence of George Aislabie, Archbishop Sterne inducted Henry Watkinson as his new Vicar-General and Official Principal.[42] He must have been glad to be rid of his turbulent Chancellor and thoroughly disillusioned by the appointment his predecessor had made.

Meanwhile the main dispute lay between Durham and York. The late summer of 1672 saw an exchange of letters between the Chapter and the Archbishop discussing the possibility of a settlement, though (one gets the impression) without much conviction on either side. On 24 July the Chapter wrote to the Archbishop acknowledging the duty they owed him in general terms but saying they were only "engaged" in the argument because of the duty they had sworn to maintain "the rights of our church". (This became a regular formula in future vacancies.) They had chosen as their Commissary someone the Archbishop would have chosen himself (*viz.* Burwell). They were sensible of the danger of public scandal and wished for a "speedy end without the noise of a public hearing, and great trouble and charge". They therefore proposed a private hearing at the next Assize in York where the Judge should hear the claims of both sides who would accept his judgement, though without prejudice for the future.[43]

Sterne replied on 29 July that he doubted Durham's rights, and as to the Vicar (Commissary) they had chosen: "I know not where you could have found a more unfit person, nor one I could have more taken exception to." Nevertheless he agreed about avoiding scandal and "therefore I like very well your proposal." He accepted the idea of a hearing at York (or perhaps at Bishopthorpe) and suggested that counsel should be engaged so that each side could understand the other's point of view.[44]

On 29 September, however, the Chapter wrote that they had heard from the bishop of Bristol (in fact one of their number) that the Archbishop wished to avoid the trouble of a King's Bench trial, scheduled for 12 November, and was suggesting a petition to the King to set up a special Commission. But, they said, it was now too late to call off the trial unless the Archbishop would agree to it being put off till the Easter term (of 1673) or to the setting up of a Commission of two or more bishops chosen by mutual agreement. A trial should be the last resort.[45]

On 3 October Sterne replied: the Chapter had misunderstood him; he wanted a decision in perpetuity, and felt that they were delaying in order to be able to continue the immediate exercise of the jurisdiction. He rehearsed past battles, especially the decision of the Delegates in York's favour, and proposed that the Chapter should remove its prohibition, and the case should go to the highest ecclesiastical court, the Archbishop meanwhile exercising the jurisdiction. Not unnaturally on 6 October the Chapter summarily rejected this proposal.[46]

Litigation was resumed. In the Michaelmas Term of 1672 Sterne appealed against the earlier prohibition at the Court of King's Bench, pleading a prescription in York's favour "time out of mind". At King's Bench "there was much evidence given, that anciently during the vacancy of Durham, the Archbishop had exercised jurisdiction, both sententious and other . . . . but since H8 (*sic*) time it had been for the most part administered by the Dean and Chapter, and the verdict here was for the Dean and Chapter".[47]

Sterne had for the moment lost. But he had one small shot left in his locker. In December and in the months that followed Francis and Thomas Parker, the Registrar of the Peculiar of Allertonshire and his assistant, were the subject of an office case in the York Chancery Court for exercising jurisdiction in the Durham Peculiar. The case started on 12 December and five days later Francis Parker denied that he had so acted or taken any fees. Thomas Parker, on the other hand, appeared and said that to avoid litigation he would return the £2 11s. he had taken in fees from wardens and on other matters; he had also granted administration on five wills. The case proceeded (though not in open court where we know Burwell might have been sitting) until 30 January 1673 when Lake, the surrogate Chancellor, took it into his own hands. Francis Parker was a senior York proctor and Registrar of one or two of the lesser York courts. He and his son knew which side their bread was buttered. Their livelihood was in York and they dared not resist even though technically the Allerton jurisdiction was now settled with Durham. There is no record of a similar situation with Howdenshire, but geographically that Peculiar on the bank of the Humber would be even more vulnerable to pressure from York.[48] Meanwhile north of the Tees during the summer and autumn of 1672 the Durham Consistory Act Books show Burwell (or his Surrogate Richard Wrench) sitting as Commissary of the Dean and Chapter *sede vacante*, and no doubt he and his surrogates were also carrying out ordinary diocesan administrative business such as institutions.[49]

In all this the leadership of Dean Sudbury was vital. On 24 July 1672 he had received the Commission of the Chapter "to treat with York about the jurisdiction *sede vacante*" and it seems that he was often on this mission in London, where he no doubt rightly judged that the action would be, leaving the Chapter to conduct day-to-day business in Durham. In November, for instance, the Sub-Dean was in charge – "the Dean being absent about the Church's business."[50]

It was Sudbury who was involved in the next imbroglio, caused by the death of Burwell in London at the end of March 1673. The King immediately issued his mandate to appoint Thomas Ireland, LL.B. to the Chancellorship *sede vacante*. But the Dean and Chapter had moved even faster. On 1 April they issued their commission to Sudbury, Richard Wrench (Burwell's regular Surrogate in the past) and Thomas Cartwright, one of the prebendaries, to exercise spiritual and ecclesiastical jurisdiction *sede vacante*.[51] On 17 June Lord Arlington, the Principal Secretary of State, wrote to the Chapter saying the King had appointed Ireland on Burwell's death "as of right he might during the vacancy of the see" until the position could be regularised on the appointment of the new bishop – the argument being, presumably, that the post was in the purview of the guardianship of the temporalities, which lay with the Crown *sede vacante*. Arlington said that the King "did not expect you to make use of any power of your own in this time of vacancy". But "on private and mean considerations" the Dean and Chapter had made their own appointments. Those appointed were required to resign so that Ireland could assume the office.[52] The Dean and Chapter were now having to defend their rights not only against the Archbishop, but against the King himself. Sudbury was equal to the task. On 27 June he addressed a long letter to Arlington. The Chapter were all "much troubled and surprised"; if Ireland has told the King he has the right to appoint "he is very much mistaken and has misrepresented us to the King." Sudbury then outlined the situation: the Chancellor is Chancellor to the Bishop, not to the Diocese, and during a vacancy the Dean and Chapter have the right and duty of a temporary commission or appointment. As Guardians of the Spiritualities they would be negligent if they failed to appoint within eight days of the former Commissary's death. Normally they appointed one or more of their own body, not the former Bishop's Chancellor; but on this occasion for special reasons Burwell had been appointed. On his death Sudbury, absent in London, had said he did not wish to be a commissioner so he had no personal or financial interest. Sudbury therefore asked for a delay to sort matters out.[53] In July Ireland took a hand. He wrote to Sudbury that he could not understand why, having appointed Burwell, they could not accept himself, especially as he had written to the Dean requesting the appointment and they had heard of the King's intention at Burwell's funeral.[54] Now it was Archbishop Sheldon's turn: on 9 September he wrote to Sudbury that, having reviewed the situation, his advice was to resign the original patent. If Ireland were sufficiently qualified it was prudent "to give all possible respect to His

Majesty's desires", especially as so many "great persons" were engaged.[55] On 12 September the matter was concluded. Cartwright had resigned the original commission and the King, though intending to appoint Ireland when the see was filled, having looked into the matter, now found that the Chapter's previous commission, and their delay in suspending it, were "solely grounded on your desire to assert your title to that office". The Chapter should therefore immediately issue its commission to Ireland *sede vacante*.[56] They might feel they had lost the battle, but they had won the war. But the war, for this vacancy, was as good as over. On 22 October 1673 Nathaniel (later Lord) Crewe was nominated to the vacant see. It had been a vacancy of exceptional length – nineteen eventful months.

There were, in fact, three aspects of the jurisdiction in the diocese *sede vacante*, or Guardianship of the Spiritualities. The first was legal – the oversight of the Consistory and other diocesan courts. There the business was disciplinary against clergy and laity, the latter mainly for sexual offences and non-attendance at church, including that occasioned by non-conformity; next there were administrative matters, such as church repairs and disputes over pews; then there was litigation between individuals, mainly tithe disputes and defamation cases; lastly there was testamentary business with its various complications. The second aspect of the jurisdiction was purely administrative, though because many of the proceedings were legal or quasi-legal they fell naturally (though not automatically) to the legally-trained Chancellor and his Registrar, who had usually served a long apprenticeship as a proctor in the diocesan courts. This was the machinery of parish resignations and institutions (excluding the bishop's patronage, which was part of the temporalities), faculties for church buildings, and licences of various sorts, especially matrimonial. All this work, legal and administrative, brought in the fees which were the bread and butter of the diocesan officials. If York established its right to the jurisdiction the fees would pass to the Archbishop's nominees to the key posts; at best if the incumbent officers were nominated the fees might be shared. At the time of the 1672 vacancy the fees, especially those reaped from court business, would have been at a reasonably high point. Later, with the decline of the courts, they would diminish.[57]

Thirdly there was a strand in the life of a diocese which could be undertaken only by a bishop – mainly ordinations and confirmations. At the King's Bench hearing in Michaelmas 1672 "Hale said, *de jure communi* the Dean and Chapter were guardians of the spiritualities . . . as to matters of jurisdiction: but for ordination they are to call on the aid of a neighbouring bishop".[58] This would usually be the case, as fee income declined, and the question of episcopal nomination became increasingly important. But on this occasion Dean Sudbury and his colleagues were in an extraordinarily strong position. One of their number was a diocesan bishop! This was Guy Carleton, who had been bishop of Bristol since 1671 but had been allowed, through the King's personal intervention, to continue to hold his prebend *in commendam* – Bristol being one of the ill-endowed Henrician bishoprics which needed this kind of arrangement to be financially viable.[59] Carleton was in fact continuing to fulfil his residence and play his part in Chapter. On 10 September 1672 he was licensed by Sudbury to conduct an ordination after Isaac Basire, the Archdeacon of Northumberland, had examined the candidates and certified their fitness, a commission which was renewed in general terms on 1 April 1673.[60]

It remains to attempt to elucidate the complex web of historical, jurisdictional and legal issues which underlay the judgement which again went in favour of Durham in 1673, and which has never been overturned. There is a mass of evidence, much of it repetitive because the lawyers and others concerned tended to re-assemble their material at each fresh vacancy. This was particularly the case with the Durham Chapter for whom the case was of paramount importance. In 1721, for instance, on Crewe's death, although the vacancy only lasted for five days before the nomination of his successor on 23 September, there was a flurry of correspondence and paperwork by the Durham lawyers, quoting the Ventris Law Report and rehearsing the Mediaeval and Tudor precedents.[61] There were, in fact, two issues when battle was joined: first the proper jurisdiction for the cause – ecclesiastical (i.e. civil) or common law courts; and second the case itself. York's position was essentially simple. The jurisdiction of a suffragan see *sede vacante* passed to the Metropolitan by universal practice in both the southern and northern provinces. If this was challenged it was an ecclesiastical matter to be tried by civil law in the church courts, that is the Court of Delegates. (A weakness of the Durham case was that in 1587 the Durham Chapter had itself initially appealed to the Delegates against the excommunication by Archbishop Sandys and by Thomas Burton, who was attempting to exercise the metropolitan jurisdiction.)[62] Once at the Delegates each side could cite Mediaeval precedents in great numbers. In the 1587 case the Hunter collection of Durham lists: evidence from 20 archbishops, 5 papal decretals, 12 royal charters and much other material in the form of sentences, letters and so on,[63] with the situation on the eve of the Reformation reflecting the compromise reached in 1286.[64] Durham would reply to this that "up to 500 years ago (from 1593) the jurisdiction lay with the Prior and Chapter" until the Pope "growing to an excessive usurpation" made the archbishops "legates for it".[65]

But Durham's case was in the event more radical and complex than this, and in the end it prevailed. Despite the fact that Durham was prepared to swap mediaeval precedents with York its claims, both as to jurisdiction and law, turned on more recent events at the Reformation and the Dissolution of the Priory of Durham, when the Prior and Convent passed to the King all their lands, privileges and jurisdictions on 31 December 1540. In turn on 12 May

1542 by letters patent the King had assigned the Durham rights and lands to the Bishop and the Dean and Chapter. On 16 May – an afterthought – the jurisdictions and privileges of the Peculiars were assigned *sede vacante* to the Dean and Chapter "as the late prior had".[66] This royal action was duly confirmed by statute.

The Durham Dean and Chapter were, therefore, able to claim – and this was the nub of their case – that the legal jurisdiction to determine their cause did not lie with the ecclesiastical courts but was "merely determinable by the common laws of England," especially as it was "a matter of inheritance and property". This was the basis of the prohibition in 1592 which was argued before the King's Bench in Westminster when York was trying to retrieve the case to the Court of Delegates.[67] There exist fuller arguments for the common law jurisdiction set out in an opinion of 1592: the case lay with the common law because the Dean and Chapter were the "immediate officers to the court to execute the Queen's will" in carrying out their duties for her and for her other courts. Moreover it lay with the Queen's court "and not the court ecclesiastical to take cognisance of all prescriptions and the confirmation of any act of parliament or letters patent". Thus when the Delegates found for York against Durham it was "to the great impeachment of the Queen's crown and dignity."[68]

These were the grounds for the prohibition from the Queen's Bench against the Court of Delegates. It was a classic early example of the competition between common and civil law courts which became more frequent in the seventeenth century. The actual arguments whereby the Queen's Bench – once the matter of jurisdiction had been settled – found for Durham are less well documented. But they are rehearsed in papers prepared for the 1672 case and preserved at Lambeth.

Both sides still appealed to ancient precedents, even though Durham also insisted that their claim rested on the fact that Henry VIII had created a new foundation and that the Dean was not the successor to the Prior.[69] Indeed, Durham was always delighted to discover examples in the southern province of other royal foundations of former abbeys which created exceptional circumstances in favour of the Dean and Chapter. Oxford was cited in 1570 and again in 1587.[70] Durham even went so far as to consider claiming that Carlisle and Chester had the same rights as Durham.[71] Against all this York could be equally far-fetched, saying that the abortive *reformatio legum ecclesiasticarum* and the eight eminent men under Cranmer appointed by Edward VI to review canon law had been on the side of the archbishop.[72] In 1672 an opinion for York listed "four things that are chiefly to be insisted on": the general custom of both provinces, the composition (presumably that of 1286), the Earl of Huntingdon's award and the 1590 sentence of the Delegates.[73] It was of no avail. Durham could counter with more recent victories. They prepared papers listing the vacancies since the 1592 common law judgement and showing that in the last six vacancies covering the past eighty years the Dean and Chapter had successfully exercised the Guardianship of the Spiritualities.[74]

It was this view which prevailed at the Court of King's Bench. The early Law Reports of Keble and Ventris unfortunately (as was the custom of the time) do not go into detail as to the arguments propounded. They list some of the legal sources cited, but only summarise the findings. Keble wrote as follows: "all agree the Archbishop hath it by common right, but the Dean and Chapter may have it by custom and usage only, which in England is generally, but not so elsewhere and verdict for the Plaintiff (*viz.* the Dean and Chapter) as to the prescription, but as to the contempt, for the Defendant, no evidence being as to that."[75] Ventris, on the final trial in the Michaelmas Term of 1672 reported that "Hale said, *De juri communi* the Dean and Chapter were guardians of the spiritualities during the vacancy of the see as to matters of jurisdiction: but for ordination they are to call on the aid of a neighbouring bishop, and so is Linwood: but the usage here in England is that the Archbishop is guardian of the spiritualities in the suffragan diocese, and therefore it was proper here to join the issue on the Usage . . . . There was much evidence given, that anciently during the vacancy of Durham the Archbishop had exercised jurisdiction: but since H8 (*sic*) time it had been for the most part administered by the Dean and Chapter: and the verdict was for the Dean and Chapter".[76] The verdict, therefore, followed the position outlined in the opinions cited above. It has never been appealed in the courts, so it stands to this day, though it has never been accepted by York.

III

The rest is coda – though a tail with a number of twists. Nathaniel, Lord Crewe had an exceptionally long reign at Durham, not dying until 18 September 1721. It was inevitable that, after nearly fifty years, the Registrar to the Dean and Chapter, Posthumous Smith, should take advice as to the position. He received two letters, dated 3 and 5 October, from William Lee, an advocate at Doctors Commons in London, rehearsing the position for him, setting out some of the mediaeval precedents, and confirming the verdicts of 1592 and 1672, with relevant quotations from Ventris.[77] Meanwhile the lists had been entered by both parties. On 26 September at Bishopthorpe the Archbishop, Sir William Dawes, issued a mandate of inhibition on the Dean and Chapter, which was served on them and on Posthumous Smith on 29, along with an inhibition on the Registrar of the Peculiar of Allerton.[78] It was accompanied by a letter of the same date in which Dawes declared his authority *sede vacante* without any reference to past events, and by another letter from his Chaplain, Thomas Sharp, to Dr Mangey, a Durham Prebendary, advising the

Dean and Chapter to "consider what they do at this junction and to take no hasty steps in this affair, but to proceed leisurely and carefully . . . and amicably with them."[79] It only took a day for the Dean and Chapter to reply: the guardianship of the spiritualities claimed by the Archbishop, "having been solemnly adjudged to us", could not be given up. They were grateful for the "tender expressions" in Sharp's letter and hoped the Archbishop would not "proceed to extremities whilst any gentle expedients can be found".[80]

The next vacancy started on 10 October 1730 after the death of Bishop William Talbot. On 13 Ralph Tutton, the Diocesan Registrar, surrendered the keys of the Registry in the Chapter House and on 15 October the Chapter issued a commission to the Dean and two Prebendaries to exercise ecclesiastical jurisdiction. This they did immediately by proceeding with institutions.[81] Their inhibition from the Consistory Court at York was dated 19 October and served on the 22 on the Dean, a Prebendary who was Official to the Dean and Chapter, and William Pye, their Registrar.[82] Thus the formula was established which persisted through thirteen vacancies from 1730 to the death of Bishop Baring in 1879. Only on one occasion did vacancies at York and Durham coincide – when Archbishop Musgrave died in 1860 and Bishop Longley was translated from Durham to succeed him. On that occasion there is no record of the Durham Dean and Chapter assuming the jurisdiction in the very short vacancy.

The ritual was duly recorded in successive Durham Chapter Act Books and York Archbishops' Registers.[83] The Dean and Chapter would move quickly on the death or translation of the Bishop. At a special Chapter meeting, usually after appropriate motions of regret at the death, they would demand the keys from the Chancellor, which would be delivered by the Registrar: only on one occasion, in 1771, did the Registrar demur. They would then appoint commissioners for the jurisdiction, at first the Dean plus two prebendaries, later the Dean plus six or seven. Episcopal jurisdiction was ignored, but the vacancies were invariably so short this would have been of no great import. In due time the Archbishop's inhibition arrived – and was disregarded. Sometimes the Chapter sent appropriate, but firm, messages of respect and regret. The Archbishops evolved their own formula for the inhibitions: the guardianship of the spiritualities was "well known to have belonged to the Archbishop" and it was his duty to defend it. In fact "it is the part and office of a good pastor to defend by penalties the jurisdiction granted by law committed to him". No one, therefore, should "presume or attempt to innovate" to York's prejudice.[84] Clearly the successive metropolitans felt that they must not let their claim lapse by default lest at any time there should be a chance of reviving it. But they went no further. No appointment of surrogates for the guardianship was attempted. The contrast with Carlisle and Chester is very marked. In 1787, for instance, there were vacancies in turn at Durham, Carlisle and Chester. Durham followed the normal pattern of a simple inhibition, duly served. Carlisle's inhibition had much the same wording. It was served on William Paley, the Carlisle Chancellor, and his Deputy Registrar on 20 August. Two days later a court entry shows Joseph Banks, the York vicar-general, appointing Paley and his surrogates as his (Banks') surrogates. It was, however, a limited jurisdiction: institutions to benefices were "accepted (*sic*) and reserved" to the Archbishop. The same procedure was followed with the Chester vacancy.[85]

This ritual served for over 150 years. But on the resignation of Bishop Charles Baring in 1879 the mould was broken. A particularly firm inhibition was served on the Dean and Chapter on 7 February and followed three days later by a special licence, and the appointment of the Chancellor as surrogate to the York Vicar-General, Sir Edmund Beckett (later Lord Grimthorpe).[86] These formal acts were accompanied by a correspondence between Archbishop Thomson and the Dean of Durham. The Archbishop wrote with his claim on 10 February and the Dean replied that he was "surprised" by this move. He referred to the previous history, saying that Durham's rights had never been challenged since the decisions made under Elizabeth, but not mentioning the 1672 litigation. He believed a "friendly interchange" would avoid litigation. There was nothing new in the situation and he could not understand a reference the Archbishop made to an Act of William IV. Thomson elucidated this in a letter the following day. The reference to William IV arose from a form of wording when the former York Peculiar of Hexham had been transferred to Durham Jurisdiction. Similarly when the diocese of Ripon had been created in 1836 the arrangements *sede vacante* had been as for all those in the metropolitan province. The Archbishop asked whether the Dean and Chapter would "bring a bishop into the Province of York without my commission". This was a significant change of emphasis: the matter of episcopal acts had become the key question. The Dean, however, had consulted Arthur Charles Q.C. who had said that the William IV legislation was irrelevant. He quoted not Ventris but a Surtees Society reference to the Durham victory after the death of Bishop Barnes, and advised that the inhibition could be ignored. This the Dean communicated to the Archbishop in a very friendly letter of 15 February: the Dean and Chapter were interested in marriage licences, faculties and institutions and would not bring in a bishop – even though Charles had said they "might" (*sic*) be able to. They were therefore proceeding to assume the spiritualities.[87]

It is difficult to see why Thomson suddenly adopted this more aggressive policy, unless he genuinely – if belatedly – thought that the legislation over Hexham and Ripon had changed the situation. But once again events aborted the controversy. Joseph Barber Lightfoot was nominated as the next Bishop on 4 March 1879 and consecrated on 25 April. It had, however, only been the curtain-raiser for what happened at his death on 26 December 1889. Warned, perhaps, by the events at the last vacancy, especially as Archbishop Thomson was still at York, the Dean and Chapter had already taken Counsel's Opinion from Francis Jeune Q.C.: "I think that the decisions of the King's Bench reported in Ventris and Keble are conclusive to show that the Dean and Chapter and not the Archbishop of York are guardians of the spiritualities *sede vacante*. The decision of the Delegates in 1590 . . . which might appear . . . to show the reverse may, I think, be explained on the supposition that the question of custom, which the ecclesiastical court could not try, was not raised."[88] The Dean and Chapter acted immediately on this, setting up a commission and appointing Jeune their Official Principal, Commissary and Vicar-General. Somewhat rashly the ex-Bishop of Tasmania was commissioned for episcopal acts with the precaution of an indemnification for him if it was proved that he was acting *ultra vires*. The Archbishop was informed and not surprisingly he responded with a prohibition. On 3 January 1890 the Durham Chapter Clerk was dispatched to London to consult Jeune. Meanwhile diocesan business was transacted. Jeune's Opinion was reported to Chapter on 6 February. He had looked further into the "somewhat obscure" proceedings of 1590 and 1672 and his opinion was confirmed. Moreover between 1592 and 1672 the Archbishop "seems to have bowed out and taken no further step . . . The Dean and Chapter exercised their jurisdiction unchallenged". Since 1672 the Dean and Chapter had "regularly" exercised their jurisdiction. His opinion was that the Archbishop "has no jurisdiction and acts by him such as ordination would be illegal and (subject to the effect of illegal episcopal ordination) invalid". The Dean and Chapter could, as Hale had said in 1672, call in a bishop, but it should be a neighbouring and not a colonial bishop.

However on the question of ordination Jeune had a compromise to suggest. The Dean and Chapter and the Archbishop could validly and without prejudice give separate commissions to an agreed bishop of the province. Then to settle the doubts Jeune suggested an action "conducted by amicable arrangement" between the parties at the Queen's Bench at which the Archbishop would be the Plaintiff. This "special case" would settle the matter once and for all. On 6 February the Chapter sent this Opinion to the Archbishop and warned him that the diocese was "suffering greatly" from the delays in confirmation and ordination. The bishops of the Province would not act against the Archbishop's wishes. Would the Archbishop, therefore, after reading the Opinion consent to a commission from the Dean and Chapter to a provincial bishop, or if he were "hesitant" would he agree to two separate commissions without prejudice? Further, they agreed with Jeune's suggestion of a trial by amicable arrangement. The delay had "retarded the work of the Church." Thomson replied that he had not had time to read the Opinion but he agreed to the proposal of two commissions. He had suggested Bishop Sandford (who was not a colonial) in January but Sandford had reported that the Archdeacon (of Northumberland) had threatened to inhibit him from acting. He therefore suggested a commission without prejudice to the Bishop of Newcastle. This the Dean and Chapter accepted, meanwhile continuing the regular diocesan administration.[89] Archbishop Thomson had not responded to the suggestion of an "amicable" trial. Perhaps he baulked at the cost. Perhaps he feared – even suspected – that he would lose!

It might have been thought that such an eminently sensible – indeed irenic – compromise would establish a precedent for the future. It did not. When Bishop Westcott died on 27 July 1901 the Chapter immediately moved in and assumed the guardianship of the spiritualities. They appointed a Commission of the Dean and six canons, with the diocesan Chancellor, Lewis Dibdin Q.C. and the Registrar, I. B. Lazenby (after he had delivered up the keys of the Registrary) to act *sede vacante*. In a brief letter they informed the Archbishop that they "had entered upon the administration of the Spiritualities of the See."[90] The matter of episcopal acts was not raised. There was no response from York. The next vacancy was in May 1920 on the death of Bishop Handley Moule. The Chapter followed the same procedure, except that the Bishop of Jarrow was one of the commissioners. He was to "ordain, consecrate and perform other episcopal acts." The Bishop accepted this charge and the Chapter agreed to indemnify him "in respect of all legal consequences and expenses which he might incur in the execution of his commission". The Archbishop, Cosmo Gordon Lang, was informed and on 22 May his Registry informed the Chapter that he said that "after giving fuller consideration to the matter (he had seen Jeune's two Opinions) he had come to the conclusion that it was not to the advantage of the see of Durham or of the metropolitan see of York that the ancient dispute between the Archbishops and the Dean . . . . should be continued". He therefore "did not propose to take any steps to assert whatever claims the Archbishop of York may have during the present vacancy".[91]

Next came the resignation of Bishop Hensley Henson on 1 February 1939: his successor, Alwyn Williams, being nominated the same day. Before this, on 25 January, Archbishop William Temple had written very formally to Dean Alington: there were doubts about the jurisdiction; the Dean and Chapter claimed it against the custom of the whole province. "Without prejudice to the general question and in order that there be no doubt as to the legality of any acts done by you during the vacancy . . . . (I) do hereby consent to recognise you as Guardian of the Spiritualities . . . during the vacancy . . . for this occasion only." If necessary he would ratify any acts of the Chapter. Here was another formula. And on 4 February, pending the full assumption of the see by Williams, both parties commissioned John Kempthorne, formerly Bishop of Lichfield, to perform episcopal acts.[92]

A new chapter began after the war on the translation of Alwyn Williams on 8 May 1952. The Diocesan Registrar, T. R. Ferens, had attended the Chapter meeting on 5 April and explained the situation. He cited the 1890 Opinion of

Sir Francies Jeune and explained the Jeune compromise which had been operated on "at least four previous occasions" – something of an exaggeration. This was the joint appointment of a bishop, the Dean and Chapter's Commission for other business, and the Chancellor authorised to deal with marriage licences and faculty applications during the vacancy. He had been in correspondence with Colonel Innes Ware, his opposite number in York, who had indicated that York would accepted this arrangement. The Chapter, therefore, nominated the Bishop of Jarrow for episcopal acts if the Archbishop had no objection. Ferens was to be "Law Officer" to the Dean and Chapter during the vacancy. Archbishop Garbett accepted the arrangement, whilst carefully safeguarding his position, and he and the Dean, John Wild, jointly appointed John Ramsbotham, Bishop of Jarrow, for episcopal acts.[93]

At the following vacancy in January 1956, when Michael Ramsey was translated to York, Ferens orchestrated the same procedure, though adding a more careful "without prejudice" clause to the formal wording. Ramsey, as Archbishop designate, agreed.[94] So again in August 1966 when Bishop Maurice Harland died. Foreseeing the event, Ferens had reported to Chapter as early as 2 April that he would prepare the deed to appoint the suffragan, which York could counter-seal "so as to make sure of the legality of the episcopal acts."[95] The vacancy of 1972 saw the same procedure, still guided by Ferens, though on this occasion three bishops were eventually chosen; Hamilton of Jarrow, Skelton, the Assistant Bishop, and John Yates, the Bishop of Whitby, a York suffragan who was at that time responsible for the Borough of Teesside, which straddled the Tees and therefore crossed the diocesan boundaries.[96]

Four co-operative compromises in a row should have established a tradition. But the old dispute did not die so easily. By September 1893, when Bishop John Habgood was translated to York, Ferens had died. The Dean and Chapter reverted to previous custom – and in a particularly aggressive manner: "in persuance of its undoubted rights to safeguard the spiritualities of the Diocese during a vacancy . . . the Dean and Chapter request and *authorise* (my italics) the Bishop of Jarrow to act on its behalf during the vacancy."[97] So at its last turn the wheel can be said to have come full circle and ealier compromises were swept aside. This can hardly have been due to the death of the irenic Ferens – and in any case Dean Eric Wild was overseeing his fourth episcopal vacancy. It may rather have been the result of new confidence and determination engendered by the defeat in Synod in 1975/6 of proposals (which will be discussed later) to centralise all jurisdiction *sede vacante*, proposals to which Durham had led the opposition. In any case the new Archbishop at York issued a commission to the Bishop of Jarrow under Section 8 of the Church of England (Miscellaneous Provisions) Measure of 1983. So effectively, instead of the previous joint commissions from York and Durham for episcopal acts, there were at this vacancy two separate and parallel commissions, it having been agreed that the York action would not prejudice the Durham claims which had been so forcibly advanced.

Finally, therefore, it must be asked: what made the dispute so protracted that it achieves a place in the *Guinness Book of Records* as the longest running unresolved legal controversy on record?[98] Some might reply the obstinacy – to use no stronger a word – of the clerical mind. This may well be true; but there are more quantifiable reasons. In the first place the issues are very complex both as to the proper jurisdiction of litigation – common or civil law – and as to the evidence and precedents concerned. This has been clearly shown in the discussion of the issues which surfaced in the 1672 trial. Secondly, the vacancies were usually so short as to preclude – unless under the "amicable" arrangements suggested by Jeune but never acted on – litigation reaching a conclusion before the issue was buried again, at least for the vacancy in question. The vacancies of 1587 and 1672 (nineteen months in the latter case) were exceptional. In the 19 vacancies from 1672 until 1972 the average time between the vacancy of the see and the nomination of the new bishop was about ten days, though two or three further months could elapse before he was fully in post.[99] Only in the two most recent appointments, those of Habgood and Jenkins, has the search for the new bishop taken as long as five months.

Thirdly there is what these days would be called the "learning curve." Most bishops had reigns of between ten and twenty years and during that time their officials (Chancellors and Registrars) changed and the old precedents had to be rediscovered. For instance, there is a note from Burwell, newly appointed in 1631, to the Dean in the vacancy between Bishops Howson and Morton. He had received the Archbishop's inhibition and commented that the Metropolitan "insists most upon a sentence against us in 1590." Clearly the Court of Delegates decision was unknown to him. The Dean was not much better briefed: "we think (*sic*) the execution of that sentence was stopped by a prohibition out of the King's Bench, for so we find it in one of our books."[100] We have seen successive Registrars retreading the same ground at the beginning of a vacancy. For some time the 1672 King's Bench judgement disappeared from view. For instance it was not quoted in Arthur Charles' Opinion in Durham's defence in 1879. Even when Jeune at the next vacancy cited it from the Law Reports of Keble and Ventris it seems that it was not his own discovery, for he acknowledged the help of a colleague. Ferens and Ware had done their homework before the vacancy of 1952, but when they disappeared from the scene their memorial did not survive them and in 1983 the Dean and Chapter reverted to the *status quo ante* and full statement of Durham's claims. The present York Provincial and Diocesan Registrar comments: "I have no personal knowledge on the matters about which you write."[101] And the present Archbishop refers to "this odd dispute" though its existence can hardly be unknown to him.[102] Perhaps it would have been better if Jeune's advice had been taken and the issue settled once and for all. Meanwhile the jury is out pending the next vacancy.

IV

There is an Epilogue, or final twist to the tail. During the vacancy of 1972, on 18 November, the Dean and Chapter as Guardians of the Spiritualities, appointed Bishop Skelton their Commissioner "to deal with a matter" under the Ecclesiastical Jurisdiction Measure of 1963, though earlier they had appointed Skelton and the Bishops of Jarrow and Whitby for episcopal acts.[103] The Ecclesiastical Jurisdiction Measure was the compendious legislation – the culmination of Archbishop Fisher's tenure of office – whereby the ecclesiastical courts were rationalised and revived and discipline thereby tightened in the Church. In the context of this study it might be felt that the reform came some three hundred years too late. The "matter" obliquely referred to must have been one of clerical discipline. The Measure also legislated for matters arising during diocesan and provincial vacancies: the church courts were not to be affected by such vacancies; disciplinary acts were to be undertaken by the person who had the Guardianship of the Spiritualities. In provincial vacancies this would be the Commissioner of the Dean and Chapter and "when a bishopric became vacant the Guardianship of the Spiritualities belongs to the Dean and Chapter of the Cathedral Church of the diocese unless by prescription or composition it belongs to the archbishop of the province".[104] In effect a rule was being enunciated which was invariably breached by all except one of the forty-one dioceses of the Church of England. Indeed, in Halsbury's section on Ecclesiastical Law the sweeping statement of the Measure is glossed – though cautiously: "in respect of most dioceses it seems that the Guardianship of the Spiritualities has by long usage been exercised by the Archbishop." These functions were the administrative ones of institutions, licences, faculties and so on. Some functions of a diocesan bishop "are, *sede vacante*, exercised by such person in episcopal orders as the Archbishop of the Province may appoint" and this rule was extended later, in 1983, to all episcopal functions.[105]

This muddled and unsatisfactory definition, in fact, did no more than reflect the confused situation outlined in the classic books of canon law. For instance, John Godolphin's post-Restoration *Repertorium Canonicum* stated that the guardianship "by Canon Law pertains to the appointment of the Dean and Chapter . . . but with us in England to the Archbishop of the Province by prescription . . . Howbeit . . . divers of the Deans and Chapters do challenge this by Ancient Charters from the Kings of this realm." Two pages later, however, Godolphin stated "the Dean and Chapter of the see is of common right the guardian of the spiritualities and not the Metropolitan", adding –

curiously – "but during the vacancy of the Bishopric of Durham the Archbishop of York is the Guardian of the Spiritualities."[106] Again, Robert Phillimore's edition of Richard Burn's eighteenth century classic *The Ecclesiastical Law* has: "by the canon law, the dean and chapter are guardians of the spiritualities during the vacancy. And it hath been allowed that of common right they are so at this day in England, and that the archbishop hath this privilege only by prescription and composition. And divers deans and chapters do challenge this by ancient charters (etc. as in Godolphin) . . . But now generally here in England . . . the archbishop is guardian . . . by prescription and composition".[107]

More recently Garth Moore's *Introduction to English Canon Law* gives the guardianship to the Archbishop of the Province with the exception that in the diocese of Durham "the Dean and Chapter claim . . . [it] . . . during the vacancy, and in fact exercise it, though the claim is formally denied by the Archbishop of York". However the general canonical rule that the guardianship belongs to the Dean and Chapter "unless it has passed to the Archbishop by prescription or composition" is repeated. (Canon C19.2)[108]

This messy situation came up for review in the General Synod in February 1975 under the Church of England (Miscellaneous Provisions) Measure passed in 1976. This Measure is something of a rag-bag intended to tidy up a number of anomalies in various aspects of the life and work of the Church. Chief among these was the matter of the Guardianship of the Spiritualities *sede vacante* which was covered in Clause 1 of the Measure. In proposing it – without, one feels on reading the debates, too much enthusiasm – Chancellor the Reverend K. J. T. Elphinstone acknowledged that "there is some doubt in certain circumstances" as to where the guardianship lay and said that the new Measure proposed to "replace all this archaic complication by a simple uniform rule". In its original form, the Clause removed the jurisdiction in Canterbury and York *sede vacante* from the Dean and Chapter (whose authority had never been challenged) and vested it in the senior Bishop of the Province – London or Winchester in Canterbury and Durham in York – or failing them in the senior bishop by appointment in the province. In dioceses the Guardianship of the Spiritualities (defined in the customary limited administrative terms) was vested in the Metropolitan during a vacancy.[109] Not surprisingly the opposition to these rationalising and centralising proposals came in the first instance from Durham. The Archdeacon of Durham, the Venerable Michael Perry, himself a member of the Durham Chapter, referred in the debate to "a quarrel with the Archbishop. This is not a particularly personal matter, because the quarrel began in the thirteenth century". Quoting precedents cited in the *Guinness Book of Records,* including the case of 1672, the Archdeacon argued that the spiritualities should be guarded "within that diocese and not by some extraneous archbishop or bishop". In fact that Canon C.19 should be adhered to, instead of the new Measure, which was "in flat contradiction to [it]".[110]

By the July session of Synod the opposition was gathering strength. Perry had been canvassing support from the Deans and Chapters which might be in the same position (as royal and statutory foundations) as Durham: that was, he believed, Canterbury and York, London, Lincoln, Exeter, Salisbury and Worcester (he might have added Oxford). He found that Canterbury and York, Durham, Salisbury and Worcester wished to re-claim their rights, while London and Exeter were "indifferent". He proposed, therefore, an amendment to Clause 1 guarding the rights of those Deans and Chapters; but this was rejected. Meanwhile a more radical amendment had been tabled; the Bishop of Chichester, Dr Eric Kemp, proposed that in *all* cases the guardianship *sede vacante* should pass to the Dean and Chapter who were to appoint a bishop or priest to exercise it – a priest being possible because it was only the administrative functions which were under consideration. This new amendment became the position of all those who were protesting at Clause 1: "the proposal before us", said Dr Kemp in the debate, "represents the climax of centuries of archiepiscopal regression (*sic*) on the independence of dioceses". The Synod Steering Committee remained committed to their proposals, but in debate Kemp's amendment was passed that month. Uniformity would be achieved, but not that envisaged by the Synod's planners.[111] In the November Group of Sessions Kemp's amendment, with minor alterations, was again carried against the "unprincipled" proposals of "centralisation".[112] Thus, after centuries of litigation which makes the York/Durham controversy the longest unsettled case in legal history the old embers had been re-ignited in Durham and had nearly led to a conflagration throughout the Church of England.

In February 1976 the Synod Steering Committee bowed to the wind and accepted the amendment but improved it with certain additions. The law officers of the diocese were to continue in post in a vacancy; provision was made for the contingency of there being a vacancy in the Deanery at the same time as that in the see; and where there was no incorporated Dean and Chapter, as in the recent foundations, the Dean (or Provost) was to appoint to the Guardianship with the Chairmen of the houses of clergy and laity of the diocesan Synod.[113]

Contemporary correspondence clarifies the issues at stake behind what were clearly somewhat confused debates. Dr Kemp's position was set out in letters of 16 and 18 January 1976 to Derek Pattinson, the Secretary-General of the Synod. Quoting Phillimore he argued that the Dean and Chapter were the "collective presbyterate" of the diocese during a vacancy. In the thirteenth century metropolitans took over the jurisdiction (an echo of seventeenth century arguments from Durham) though some Deans and Chapters resisted; at the Council of Trent their position had been vindicated. There was "a strong case for returning to the ancient canonical principle of locating the guardianship firmly in the diocese." The Tridentine arrangement whereby the Dean and

Chapter appointed one person – the Roman Catholic vicar-capitular – would be preferable to a multiple commission. With the centralising practice there was "tremendous duplication," more work, especially for the archbishops, and a loss of fees to the dioceses. (This was presumably a reference to the fact that in the southern province all the fees *sede vacante* were taken by the provincial officials, whereas in the northern they were shared between the diocesan and the provincial offices.)

The "official" position is set out in a letter of 14 July 1975 when the Canterbury Provincial Registrar, David Moir Carey wrote to the Synod Revision Committee, requesting a meeting: a lessening of the burdens on Archbishops and their Registrars would certainly be welcome but "the Bishop's (*viz*. Kemp's) proposals just will not work in practice in the vast majority of dioceses". It is not "control from Lambeth or Bishopthorpe"; normally the archbishops appoint the guardians, usually suffragans or archdeacons, to administer the vacant diocese and then "drop out". It is not true that the present custom, to be enshrined in the new canon, leads to duplication.

In the event both the original clause 1 and Kemp's amendment to it – radically opposing models for achieving uniformity in church practice – were dropped for lack of time in Synod proceedings. It was, as Pattinson said, a "draw". Indeed it was a goal-less draw. By default the *status quo ante* was resumed. Technically the canon law remains that of Canon C19, 1. The guardianship in a metropolitan vacancy falls to the Dean and Chapter (C19, 1.); in a bishopric "the guardianship of the spiritualities belongs to the Dean and Chapter of the Cathedral Church of the diocese unless by prescription or composition it belongs to the archbishop of the province, acting by or through such person or persons as he may nominate according to the prescription or composition."[114] Custom and practice dictate that the major premise of the canon is ignored in all but one of the forty-one non-metroplitan dioceses of the Church of England. Uniquely Durham maintains the basic canonical position it last defended in 1672.

Notes to text

1   E. O. A. Whiteman, 'The Re-establishment of the Church of England, 1660-1663'
     Transactions of the Royal Historical Society, 5 Series, 5 (1955) p. 117.

2   For the text of the Worcester House Declaration see A. Browning, *English Historical
     Documents, 1660-1715* (1966) pp. 365-370. George Gould, *Documents relating to the
     Settlement of the Church of England by the Act of Uniformity of 1662* (1862) is not to be relied
     on as he omits the "small print" tightening the force of the Declaration at the end of almost
     every section, which were exactly the last minute additions which so delighted and surprised
     Baxter. For the text of the original draft see *Reliquiae Baxterianae*, pp. 259 ff.

3   Baxter would have preferred to bid for more at Worcester House, including no doubt the
     reform of the ecclesiastical courts but he was restrained by his colleagues, who thought it safer
     to stick to Ussher.

4   W. Cobbett *Parliamentary History of England*, 4 (1808) pp. 151 ff.

5   This was not, as William Bates said in his funeral oration on Baxter's death, because of the
     king's 'averseness' to Worcester House itself, but because for him such new arrangements for
     the Church were a matter, not for Parliament, but at least for Convocation, or preferably
     for the royal prerogative: Bates, *Works* (2 ed. 1723) p. 816.

6   R. S. Bosher, *The Making of the Restoration Settlement*, (1956) p. 196. Recent surveys of the
     restoration of the Church of England start with Bosher, but have been revised by I. M. Green
     The Re-establishment of the Church of England, 1660-1663, (1978). Green sees the Settlement
     as the product, not so much of the careful orchestration of the "Laudians", as of other
     conservative forces in church and society. This view is followed by Ronald Hutton *The
     Restoration, 1658-1667*, (Oxford 1985), Paul Seaward *The Cavalier Parliament and the
     Reconstruction of the Old Regime, 1661-1667*, (Cambridge 1989) and John Spurr *The
     Restoration Church of England, 1646-1689*, (Yale 1991). The present writer hopes to publish
     a further study of the Worcester House Declaration, and the reasons for its stillbirth.

7   Ronald Marchant *The Church under the Law* (Cambridge 1969) p. 227.

8   Spurr, *Restoration*, p. 39; B[orthwick] I[nstitute], PK 155; B. D. Till, 'The Ecclesiastical
     Courts of York, 1660-1883: A Study in Decline' (unpublished MS lodged at B[orthwick]
     I[nstitute]) pp. 2 ff.

9   Till, 'Courts of York' p. 10.

10   All dates are given new style. Lake was writing from his house in Chancery Lane, London.
     He wrote in warm personal terms, sending his and his wife's "love" to Combes and his wife,
     and signing himself "your very loving friend." In the first letter of the series, on 12 August
     1660, he was concerned to instruct Combes about his new style as a baronet. He had been
     a committed Royalist in the Civil War, receiving no less than sixteen wounds at the Battle
     of Edgehill. The King had commented: "for a lawyer, a professed lawyer, to throw off his
     gown and fight so heartily for me, I must needs think very well of it". Hence the baronetcy,
     though he did not collect it till the Restoration: 'Sir Edward Lake's Account of his Interviews
     with Charles I';, ed. T. P. Langmead (Camden Miscellany, 1859). At the Restoration he
     asked for preferments and land, but had to be content with the Chancellorship of Lincoln
     diocese. In 1662 he wrote a defence of the *ex officio* oath: *D.N.B.* The series of letters is in
     Nottingham University Library: Nottingham Archdeaconry, M.254 (Misc).

11   C[alendar of] S[tate] P[apers] D[omestic], Charles II] 19, p. 323.

12   Marchant, *Church under Law* p. 83, note 3. Till, 'Courts of York" p. 4. Aislabie very rarely
     appeared in person in the courts, though his frequent signatures on official documents show
     that he attended his office. He was eventually killed in a duel in the streets of York after
     church on Sunday, 10 June 1675: Till, 'Courts of York' p. 23. Aislabie was the father of John
     Aislabie who, after his disgrace as Chancellor of the Exchequer in the South Sea Bubble,
     retired to the family estate at Studley Royal where he laid out the magnificent formal gardens.

There is a portrait of John Aislabie, who was not born till 1670, at Beningbrough Hall.

13   There was, in fact, at least one precedent for the Chancellorships of York and Durham being held by the same man. William Easdall was concurrently in the two posts from 1628 to 1632. There was presumably some special reason for this arrangement, but he resigned the Durham post in 1632 no doubt at the behest of Archbishop Richard Neile. As a former Bishop of Durham, before a brief sojourn at Winchester from 1628 to 1631, Neile would have had good reason to know the undesirability of the two posts being held in tandem. Easdall was the chief and trusted official of Neile: Marchant, *Church under Law*, p. 48; Patrick Collinson, *The Religion of the Protestants*, p. 64; Brian P. Levack, *The Civil Lawyers in England, 1603-1641*, p. 227.

14   Venn, *Alumni Cantabrigienses*, part 1, (1922) p. 269; B. D. Henning, *The House of Commons, 1660-1690* (History of Parliament Trust) 1, pp. 752 ff; *The Chronology of Certain Eminent Persons* (MS in Dr Williams' Library, London) p. 4. On his arrival in York Burwell was appointed to the Commission which was overseeing the restoration of the temporalities of the see, along with (among others) Aislaby, who was the Receiver General. This was a typical example of the place of the Chancellor as a (if not the) senior official in the archdiocese: W. J. Sheils, 'The Restoration of the Temporalities: Archbishop Frewen's Commissioners, 1661-1662' *Borthwick Institute Bulletin*, I, (1975) p. 21.

15   BI, HC.CP.ND/12, R VII PL 138. The Articles are drawn in such a way as to indicate that this had been a regular practice of Burwell's over the past six years, i.e. since going to Durham. Burwell is referred to as Chancellor of Durham, but a similar set of Articles against Thomas Bullock, the Registrar of the Peculiar of Allerton, makes it clear that the offences had been taking place there, and Burwell was taking the rap, even though Arthur Hutton was his deputy Official in Allerton. Hutton and Bullock held various posts in the Durham diocese, whereas for geographical reasons the Howden Peculiar courts tended to be staffed by officers from the York courts. David Marcombe, 'The Dean and Chapter of Durham 1558-1603' (unpublished Ph.D. Thesis, Durham University) p. 215. The Articles, which under Canon Law could have led to the Chancellor's suspension,were counter-signed by Edward Mottershed, the King's Advocate in the North. Bullock was accused of continuing to aid and abet the Chancellor's practices even after Burwell had been questioned in the High Commission: Marchant, *Church under Law* p. 250; Levack, *Civil Lawyers* p. 257. For the Peculiars as a source of friction between York and Durham in the Middle Ages, see R. B. Dobson, *Durham Priory, 1400-1450* (Cambridge, 1973) p. 215.

16   Marcombe, 'Durham' p. 220 and references.

17.   *Ibid*. pp. 219 & p. 221 ff.

18   The Court of Delegates did not sit permanently, but as constituted anew for each appeal with a bench of judges appropriate to the matter in hand. In a cause of this importance the delegates were suitably prestigious, comprising the Bishops of London and Rochester, the Lord Chief Justices of the King's Bench and the Court of Common Pleas, a Master of Requests, the Attorney General, a Judge of the Court of Admiralty, and only one member of Doctors Commons: Marcombe, 'Durham' pp. 225-231.

19   *Ibid*. p. 222.

20   In legal usage prescription is defined as "uninterrupted use or possession from time immemorial" and "the title or right acquired by this" . . . "Ancient custom . . . viewed as authoritative." *O.E.D.*

21   Dobson, *Durham* p. 218.

22   *Ibid*. See also Marcombe, 'Durham' p. 213 ff.

23   *Ibid*. p. 219. And see also the notes on procedure throughout the Middle Ages made by Prior Wessington. The mediaeval tradition is discussed in R. Brentano 'Late Medieval Changes in the administration of vacant suffragan sees: province of York', *Yorkshire Archaeological Journal*, 38 (1952-5) pp. 496-503.

24   Dobson, *Durham* p. 222. A further cause of dispute in the Middle Ages was over who enthroned a new Bishop of Durham; the Archdeacon of York claimed the right against the Prior, though unsuccessfully. *Ibid*. pp. 228 ff.

25   Marcombe, 'Durham' p. 215, quoting D[urham] U[niversity] L[ibrary, Mss. collections], Dean and Chapter Register C, f. 132.

26   *Ibid*. pp. 215-219.

27   *Ibid*. pp. 232-238. Marcombe gives the date of the sentence as 16 February 1590; but a Durham copy of the sentence has the date 30 December (DUL, Misc Ch 6818c), while a Lambeth copy, made at the order of Charles II for the 1672 case about to be considered, gives 3 December 1590. (Lambeth, MS 3403, f. 128). In any case the Hunter MSS in the Chapter Library show that the case was active and moving towards sentence in June and July, 1590. (Durham, CL, Hunter 32 f. 21v & 22r.)

28   Coke was to lead the attack on the ecclesiastical courts which came to a head between 1604 and 1607, when Archbishop Bancroft appealed to the King to protect the spiritual jurisdiction. He and the King claimed that the Monarch could alter boundaries of jurisdiction by his royal prerogative – a position which led to a direct confrontation between the King and the Common Lawyers: J. D. Eusden, *Puritan Lawyers and Politics in Early Seventeenth Century England* (Yale 1958) pp. 89-94. For the actual procedure by which secular courts inhibited ecclesiastical, see Levack, *Civil Lawyers* pp. 73 ff.

29   DUL, Misc Ch. 6818 & 5902.

30   The reference to the Northumberland jury is in a letter of 5 October 1721 from William Lee, an advocate working for Durham, to Posthumous Smith, the Registrar to the Dean and Chapter: DUL, D & C, Loose Papers 22.

31   DUL, Misc Ch. 6818d. This is an Opinion summarising the situation at each of the ten vacancies from Tunstall's deprivation in 1553 to the Restoration when, both sees being vacant, the Dean and Chapter set up a Commission for the jurisdiction and effected "divers institutions". Given these dates the Opinion, which answers questions about the common and civil (i.e. canon) law and the attitudes of the Archbishops, must have been prepared in the 1672 controversy.

32   DUL, D & C, Loose Papers 22. No pagination.

33   DUL, Misc Ch. 6818d.

34   York Minster Library, Dean and Chapter Act Book, H4, f. 651. The vacancy of 1632 was also a double one and on 20 February the York Dean and Chapter are found instituting to the Rectory of Ford, Northumberland, at the presentation of the patron. But whether the institution was effected is not known; *Ibid*. f. 713.

35   DUL, Dean and Chapter Act Book, 1660-1688, no pagination.

36   BI, Abp. Reg. 33, 1660-1713, ff. 113 ff. Lambeth MS 3403 f. 129 says the case was heard in the Minster but it is more likely that Sterne would have removed the cause to a hearing *in camera*.

37   BI, Abp. Reg. 33, f 113 ff. An Opinion at Durham (DUL, Misc Ch. 5902) confirms the various dates. The Dean and Chapter were asking whether they should appeal to the Court of Delegates or move for a King's Bench prohibition, and in which order. The proceedings at King's Bench are recorded in two very early Law Reports: Joseph Keble, *Reports in the Court of King's Bench* 3 (1685) pp. 17 & 28, and *The Reports of Sir Peyton Ventris, Kt* 1 (1726 edn.) p. 234.

38   BI, Cons. AB 80, p. 103.

39   *Ibid. ad diem.*

40   BI, Cons. AB 79, flyleaf note at the end of book.

41   B. D. Henning, *The House of Commons 1660-1690*, p. 753.

42   BI, Cons. AB 81, flyleaf entry at front of book.

43   DUL, D & C, Loose Papers 22, no pagination.

44 *Ibid.*
45 *Ibid.*
46 *Ibid.*
47 *The Reports of Sir Peyton Ventris, Kt* 1 (1726 edn.) p. 225.
48 BI, Abp. Reg. 33, ff. 121r, 123v & 124.
49 For example: DUL, D & C, Dean and Chapter Court Acts, 1662-1672 (SJB/3 p. 44, 11 September 1672) and Consistory Court Act Book, 1666-1674 (Durham University Library, DDR III.15) 27 September 1672 and throughout January 1673.
50 DUL, Chapter Act Book, 1660-1688. No pagination.
51 *Ibid.*
52 *Ibid.* and *CSPD*, 1 March-31 October 1673 (1902) p. 377.
53 DUL, D & C, Loose Papers 22; Chapter Act Book, 1660-1688, *CPSD* p. 397.
54 *CSPD* p. 472.
55 DUL Chapter Act Book, 1660-1688.
56 DUL, D & C, Loose Papers 22, Chapter Act Book, 1660-1688, *CSPD* p. 543. On 15 October Ireland assumed his position in the Consistory Court, and confirmed the proceedings in cases before the court *iuxta forma retroactorum*: D.D.R. III.15. *op.cit.ad. diem.* See also C. E. Whitney, *Nathaniel Lord Crewe, Bishop of Durham*, pp. 72 ff.
57 This very abbreviated summary of the legal and administrative jurisdiction of a diocese is based on the writer's 'Courts of York'.
58 Ventris, *Reports* I p. 225.
59 DUL, Chapter Act Book, 1660-1688. Carleton, like Sir Edward Lake, was another Royalist with, for a man of his cloth, a dashing war record, including escaping from captivity at Lambeth with the help of his wife. After that he joined the King in Holland and was rewarded with the Deanery of Carlisle at the Restoration. This past history accounted, no doubt, for the King's protection of his Durham prebend and in turn for Carleton being unwilling to oppose the King's wishes in the Durham Chapter.
60 DUL, D & C Act Book, 1660-1688.
61 DUL, D & C Loose Papers 22. Eight letters in September and October 1721, with accompanying papers. It is noticeable that the bulk of the evidence preserved comes from Durham – with an important exception from Lambeth. This may be because archival papers at Bishopthorpe were destroyed; or it may be that the issue was for the Durham Dean and Chapter the most important with which they had to deal, whereas for the Archbishop of York it was one of many. Nevertheless some Opinions and arguments in favour of York were preserved at Durham.
62 Lambeth [Palace Library], MS 3403 f. 190, Marcombe, 'Durham' pp. 233 ff.
63 Durham, D & C, Hunter MSS 32.
64 Dobson, *Durham* p. 218; c.f. Lamberth MS 3403 f. 140; and see above p. 5.
65 Lambeth, MS 3403 f. 164. The Lambeth MS preserves papers and opinions from 1672 favouring each side. It would be natural that Archbishop Sheldon would wish to acquaint himself with the arguments in so important a case. Indeed the first paper in the collection is a copy of the Delegates' sentence of December 1590 made on the instructions of the King himself by Thomas Oughton, the Principal Registrar of the Court of Delegates and author of *Ordo Judiciorum*, one of the classic books on procedure in the ecclesiastical courts.
66 Lambeth, MS 3403 f. 139, also ff. 170-201 which is Durham's case for the 1590 Prohibition. The word of the king's action at the foundation of the Chapter is "reddidit". The same ground is retraced in BL, Harl 6853 f. 156 and Durham, D & C Hunter MSS 11, ff. 125 & 126 which was producing precedents for the 1672 dispute.
67 DUL, Misc Ch. 5902.
68 BL, Harl 6853 f. 154.
69 Durham, D & C Hunter MSS 11 f. 126, and Misc Ch. 5902 'The Case of the Dean and

Chapter v. The Archbishop of York', 1672.

70   Durham, D & C Hunter MSS 32 f. 59r and Marcombe 'Durham' pp. 217 & 227.

71   Lambeth, MS 3403 f. 199.

72   DUL, D & C Loose Papers 22, in an Opinion for the Archbishop, probably at the 1771 vacancy.

73   Lambeth, MS 3403 f. 153.

74   *Ibid*.; Durham, D & C Hunter MSS 11 f. 126; Misc Ch. 6818 is a similar Opinion prepared in 1672 and going back to Tunstall's deprivation. It concludes: 'in fact we have 40 years which is sufficient prescription against his.'

75   Joseph Keble, *Reports in the Court of King's Bench*, 3 (1685) p. 91.

76   Ventris, *Reports* 1 p. 225.

77   DUL, D & C Loose Papers 22; Letters of 3 & 5 October 1721.

78   BI, Abp. Reg. 34 f. 145r.

79   DUL, D & C Loose Papers 22.

80   *Ibid*. and (for the full text) BI, Bishopthorpe Papers, Bp C & P II/23.

81   DUL, Dean and Chapter Act Book, 1729-1777, *ad diem*.

82   BI, Abp. Reg. 35 f. 99v.

83   The relevant Dean and Chapter Act Books at Durham are those for: 1729-1777, 1778-1796, 1819-1829 (Shute Barrington having had a long reign from 1791 to 1826), 1829-1838, 1847-1856, 1857-1876, 1876-1890. The York Archbishops' Registers are Nos. 35-38.

84   BI, Abp. Reg. 46 f. 942, the 1879 vacancy.

85   *Ibid*. 38, ff. 189v, 190 & 193.

86   *Ibid*. 46, ff 942, 943 & 945.

87   DUL, Dean and Chapter Minute Book, 1879-1890.

88   *Ibid*.

89   *Ibid*. In both these disputes the correspondence is preserved, along with the record of formal acts, in the Chapter Minute (or Act) Book. At the York end there is very little documentation beyond the formal inhibitions and the certificates of their having been served. In both disputes there were licences to the Chancellor of Durham (Jeune in the 1889 case) to grant marriage licences as the surrogate of Beckett/Grimthorpe: BI, Abp. Reg. 46 p. 945 & 48 p. 708).

90   DUL, Dean and Chapter Act Book, 1898-1905.

91   *Ibid*. 1916-1929, pp. 138 & 142.

92   BI, Abp. Reg. 51, pp. 244f; DUL, Dean and Chapter Minute Book, 1939-1947, p. 7.

93   BI, Abp. Reg. 52, pp. 295 ff; Durham, Dean and Chapter Minute Book, 1947-1953, pp. 252 ff. For the election of Ramsey the Dean and Chapter appointed two London legal proctors plus Ware and Ferens.

94   Durham, Dean and Chapter Minute Book, 1954-1958, p. 164.

95   *Ibid*. 1965-1969 p. 98. The Commission was sealed on 1 September.

96   *Ibid*. 1970-1974, pp. 215, 222 & 228. I owe the explanation of the appointment of the Bishop of Whitby to Canon Michael Perry.

97   *Ibid*. 1982-1984, p. 651. Canon Perry has once again provided me with helpful information on the 1983 vacancy.

98   *Guinness Book of Records* (1993 edition) p. 184. The dispute is listed under 'the most protracted litigation' and cites the cases of 1283, 1672 and 1890.

99   Ed. E. B. Fryde, D. E. Greenway, S. Porter & I. Roy, *A Handbook of British Chronology* (Third Edition) p. 243. In fact the exact dates given can often be faulted by reference to, for example, the Dean and Chapter Minute Books; but the fact of short vacancies remains the same.

100   DUL, Dean and Chapter, Loose Papers, 22.

101   Letters to the Author, 20 January 1993.

102   Letter to the Author, 5 January 1993.

103 DUL, Dean and Chapter Minute Book, 1970-1974, pp. 228, 215 & 222.
104 *Halsbury's Statutes. 14. Ecclesiastical Law* (4 Edn. 1986) pp. 289 & 323.
105 *Ecclesiastical Law* (General Synod Edition, Halsbury 4 Edn., 1975) p. 235, para. 488. *Halsbury's Statutes* (4 edn.), 14, p. 471.
106 John Godolphin, *Repertorium Canonicum, or an Abridgement of the Ecclesiastical Laws of this Realm* (3 Edn. 1689) pp. 39 & 41.
107 Richard Burn, *The Ecclesiastical Law* (9 Edn. 1842) 1 p. 225.
108 E. Garth Moore, *Introduction to English Canon Law* (Oxford 1967), p. 28. Garth Moore was Chancellor of Durham at the time, and of other dioceses. See also *Moore's Introduction to English Canon Law*, ed. Timothy Briden & Brian Hanson (3 edn. 1992) p. 27.
109 General Synod, February 1975, *Report of Proceedings,* Vol. 6, No. 1, pp. 234·ff.
110 *Ibid.* p. 242.
111 *Ibid.* Vol. 6. No. 2, pp. 377.
112 *Ibid.* Vol. 7. No. 1, pp. 116 & 120.
113 *Ibid.* Vol. 7. No. 2 February 1976, pp. 466 ff.
114 *Canons* (of 1964, 1969 & 1970) (4 Edn. 1986), p. 82.